Through the Looking Glass: A Collection of Poetic Reflections

Sparsh Verma

Through the Looking Glass: A Collection of
Poetic Reflections © 2023 Sparsh Verma

All rights reserved.

No part of this publication may be
reproduced, stored in a retrieval system, or
transmitted, in any form or by any means,
electronic, mechanical, photocopying,
recording or otherwise, without the prior
written permission of the presenters.

Sparsh Verma asserts the moral right to be
identified as author of this work.

Presentation by *BookLeaf Publishing*

Web: www.bookleafpub.com

E-mail: info@bookleafpub.com

ISBN: 9789357745420

First edition 2023

DEDICATION

To my wife Tanya, my parents, Subodh & Asha
and my in-laws Rakesh & Sunita, Aakash &
Shikha.

ACKNOWLEDGEMENT

- Amat Victoria Curam -

I would like to take this opportunity to express my gratitude to all the people who have helped me on my journey to trying my hand at becoming a writer and publishing this collection of poems, "Through the Looking Glass: A Collection of Poetic Reflections."

Firstly, I want to thank my parents, Subodh and Asha, for always supporting me and believing in my dreams. Their unwavering love and encouragement have been a constant source of inspiration for me.

I would also like to express my heartfelt gratitude to my wife, Tanya, for her love, support, and patience during this journey. Her belief in me has been a driving force in my pursuit of writing. Every time I faltered, gave up belief, she brought it upon herself to ensure I got back on the right track.

My friends, Shashank, Avani, Saurabh and Roser, have been an integral part of my journey, providing constant support and encouragement along the way.

I also want to acknowledge the role of my teachers and professors who recognized my talent for writing and nurtured it from an early age. Their guidance and support have been instrumental in helping me develop my literary skills.

Lastly, I want to thank all the readers who have taken the time to read my work and appreciate it. Your support and encouragement mean the world to me.

O Mannequin!

O Mannequin, You beautiful one!
 Glistening in the gleam of these bright lights.

 Rolls of soft muslin scattered by your feet
 And the aroma of a hundred rose petals
 Elegantly surround you on all sides,
 Draped in the finest fabrics men have ever seen
 You magnificently stand tall, shimmering,
 In the opulence of luxury where you reside.

 Whilst a hungry child looks upon yearnfully,
 At thy grandiosity from the street outside
 Braving the pangs of hunger and the wrath of
sunshine,
 He stands barefoot, admiring your boots.
 His ragged robe not holding a candle to thy
silken vests
 And all his dreams drowned deep in the
moonshine.

 Unable to withstand your scent of roses & lilies
 His dejected despairing eyes get constantly
blinded with
 Your glimmer of beatitude reflecting through
the glass panes

O Mannequin, how could you be so deprived of shame?
Or is it us, We Humans, who for his sufferings, are to blame?

A Hazy Reality

Is this life real, or just a myriad of echoing
wailing voices,
 That conjure up an apparition made of shattered
dreams.
 Is it worth walking on the sword, fiddling
between the choices?
 Hoping the mere agony of existence would help
one redeem.

 Is the Sun actually shining brightly in the skies
 Or it's a beautiful illusion the mind creates to
shun darkness away.
 Do the birds still sing melodies or remind us of
our unending lies
 That we secretly buried in the past to believe in
a better today.

 Does the river still sparkle with the blue
reflection of heaven?
 Or our unending materialistic lust has turned it
all red.
 Have our sins increased manifold surpassing
that number seven
 And do we realize now we have become the
very monsters under our bed.

Slumber's Alibi

I see rows of red flowers blooming brightly in
the sun.
 Or are they just white tulips drenched in my
blood?
 Standing on the bridge, silent, and in a mess
 I see my hopes helplessly sink below in the
mud.

 I walk down the streets, feeling lost in the
dusk's crowd.
 More than their cacophony, my silence screams
loud
 As night came closer, I heard those church bells
toll.
 And the reflection in my mirror dug its fangs in
my soul.

 I lay on the bed, hopelessly gazing at the broken
lamps.
 The voices in my head ring louder than that
faint lullaby.
 Sleep evading me once again to wander in the
bright nights
 Concocting up tales it hears around to give me
her alibi.

"It will pass", "Cheer up man", "It's all in your mind"
"Think positive. The day is so bright", "look at the rainbow above"
But nobody stops to lend a hand and understand
With depression, you stop loving the things you love.

The Sea has a Story to Tell

If you ever decide to walk down the jungle roads
 Passing under the trees where barbets dwell
 And settle down on those quiet sandy beaches,
 You'll know that the sea has a story to tell.

 It will tell you how it's waves crashed upon the
shore
 Listening to the music that the seashells sang
 The footprints in the sand murmured tales
furtively
 While in the background, distant church bells
rang.

 On the quieter days the sea would wait & listen
 To that lonely person who sat on the rocks
crying
 There were moonlight nights when the sea
overheard
 The promises of love from the couple on the
beach, lying.

 It had felt the unsteady footsteps of a toddler
splashing
 It had sensed the firm stride of a man deciding
to drown

It had been the fiend that deluged boats in its
fury
It had been docile, playing with inflated ducks
like a clown.

All the sea wants is for you to come by on a
sunny day
Sit on the beach, listening to its story while
sipping your wine
Share its laughter while you jump in, taking a
dip of faith
Shed a tear, reminiscing the days gone by, as the
moon shines.

Her Touch

Waiting
Year after year
For her magical touch
To heal all his sore open wounds
Again

Walking
All by himself
Hopelessly, Aimlessly
Bearing the weight of his demons
Alone

Wishing
She was with him
Holding tightly his hands
Whilst he bravely fought off this world
O' Ma!

What You Lost

Have you ever sat down alone on your old
home's floor
 Gazing reminiscently into the empty walls
around
 Wishing the past would walk in right through
the door
 And this deafening silence would fill with love
and sound.

 Have you ever dusted away those old squeaky
toys
 Whose funny noises once echoed through your
home
 Rediscover the almirahs where you hid with
other boys
 Walk again in the flowery gardens you once
used to roam.

 Have you ever flipped through the thumbed
pages of the book
 Within which you hid the roses she gave one
valentine
 Rustled through the worn out photos of her that
you took

In the days when all you had was love without a
penny or a dime.

 And today when you stand all alone in this
emptiness
 Shoulders weighed down by all the glories you
have earned
 You realize all along you were just chasing an
illusion of happiness,
 It was that lost childhood for which your heart
always yearned.

The Three Day Old Bread

A broken cane in his hand
Some shattered dreams in his eyes
He hobbled slowly veiling his wounds.
Searching for the promised land
where hope never dies.

He had spun some dreams of his own
Some he was made to believe in by the world.
Those turned out to be lies and deceit,
His own dreams were crushed bearing the
weight
Of the hard-hearted callousness of the same
world.

He kept his shield up, braving the apathy
Fighting the savagery every step of his life.
The poor man knows his life to be a challenge
Where every day he has to walk barefoot
On an infinitely perilous bed of knife.

Days after trudging through streets of sorrow
Streets where every rest stop reeks of despair
He came across a flourishing villa

With grass that was green and water that shone blue
For him which was a sight so rare.

He saw a child, toddling his way through the gardens.
A glimpse so beautiful, it made him smile.
Moving his attention to the rubbish bin outside the house
He dove in, to find something to eat
Despite the fact the bin smelt vile.

He sat down near the gates, holding a stale bread.
His victor's treasure he had scavenged from the waste.
Just as he took his bite, a lovely voice surprised him
"Don't eat that bread it's three days old
It will have a very foul taste."

He looked up and saw it was that child.
Staring at him with a dumbfounded disbelief
He smiled at him and said
"The bread may be three days old, but my hunger is four
And even the foul taste gives me relief."

The child knelt down and looked at him
And reached his hand out to touch the dirt
caked face
Only to be interrupted by a voice screaming
"Get away from that filthy poor man"
And yanked away to be inside the luxuries of
the space.

The man sat down resting his tired back against
the wall
Chewing through the stale hard bread and
smiling whilst,
Looking up to the sky.
"You may think that this bread is rotten and
stale
But have You ever looked at their empty eyes
Some say that You made them in Your own
image
If only I was naive enough to believe in these
lies."

The Lost Warmth

A cold wind once blew in the streets
 Scattering his unkempt hair

Across his haggard face
Making his visage appear
Messier than any normal day.

The frigid frosty air he inhaled
Scarred his lungs with every breath
His lips chafed & turned ruddier.

Every time he yelled out her name
His cold sore voice was too weak to be heard.
Across the snug warmth of her window panes.

Where she sipped leisurely on her hot wine
 Whilst he languished knee-deep in the snow
 His soul holding onto the memories of old
times.

Deliverance

Tell me something which you may have told
none,
 like when very morning, the first rays of the
Sun
 break your slumber pirouetting on your cheek,
 That moment, what's that one sole thing, which
you seek?

 Is it waking up and heading to work like any
other day?
 Or skipping everything to lie down on the sand
by the bay?
 Maybe stroll down the memory lane to see who
all you have missed
 The boys with whom you pranked the girl you
once had kissed.

 Racing against time chasing dreams that aren't
truly yours
 Cancelling hanging out with friends to meet
some deadlines.
 Stowing away that passion which lights up your
eyes

To just look back one day, wistfully regretting
all these lost times.

 Life's only a span of some years, broken into
months and days
 For you to pace around and achieve in a
multitude of ways
 Collecting gems scattered around the path,
carefully knowing what they mean.
 And cherish the joy the heart feels when you
fulfil your dreams.

Nothing , Nowhere

Some tell me I am not a good son.
 I say I was never considered a good son.
 Then, when those people went away,
 My friend, my only friend, held my hand & told me
 That I never ever tried to become a good son.

"Oh Yes" I said when he said So
I told him that he should understand
that the last time I saw my father….
He stopped me in between and told
"It's the last time I went to see my father."

I repeated nonchalantly after him,
That the last time I went to see my father,
He asked how my life was going along.
I looked out of the window tapping my feet
My father smiled and told me that he understood
I might have someone more important to meet.

"Oh Yes?" My friend stared at me and asked
I looked away towards the leaves falling down
 Yes I said, it was someone I could not keep waiting

and I told my father it was so, wearing a frown
 My father sighed, holding my arm with his cold
hands
 I would want you to stay but would not delay
your errands.

 "Oh Yes! I Know!" He said "Your father told
me so!"
 My friend tried to hold my hand. I said no.
 I closed my eyes and remembered that night
 "Do You want to know something that only I
Know?"
 "Oh Yes" he said
 "There was nothing I had to do
 There was nowhere I had to go…"

An Evanesced Sketch

I wish they would never come to me,
 eyes glittery and their souls full of glee.
 Reaching out, giving me their hands,
 and ask me to paint a picture of thee.

I would have to get up and clean these clothes,
 to shrug off this dirt like one sheds away tears.
 Frisk around to realize the paintbrush was gone,
 Just like this soul had been lost for years.

An artist am I, would never let them down,
 I would scrape my fingers till they dripped of
red.
 I would draw your visage on the black of the
void,
 across the horizons of my sight, which spread.

Every stroke would sap the blood from my
fingers,
 Like slowly this heart exsanguinated with your
lack.
 Every detail of your smile would gradually
grow feeble,

And just like my dreams, eventually fade to
black.

But they would applaud every scarlet drop that
drained,
Cheer for every tear that trickled down the face.
Mere an artist I am, owing fealty to their mirth,
The tragedies of my soul; their ebullience and
grace.

An Unfinished Tale

She is a beautiful girl,
 with a pair of sparkling eyes.
 Her eyes tell a story,
 different from what to all she lies.

She had a lot of dreams and
 weaved them to form a picturesque life.
 But fate had different plans
 inflicting her life with sorrow and strife.

She wanted to fly away
 to a land full of happiness & grace.
 But life kept on giving her blemishes,
 which she had to sadly embrace.

I stand aside and look at her,
 lost in the sublimity of her alluring visage.
 I see the sorrow she carries in her eyes,
 while others get lost in the resplendent mirage.

I want to get down on my knees
 & collect the shards of her broken dreams.
 No matter if those pieces lacerate my hands
 I want to ornate them into meaningful themes.

I know I am a dreamer,
But it's long since I have been awake.
I have no dreams of mine
it's hers true that I want to make.

I stand near the rock on which she sits
lost in the thoughts of the dreams that broke.
I look at her & I wish with a sigh that I could
brighten her life with colourful paint strokes.

A Monster Unmasked

I was tired of sleeping under your bed.
 It was then when I decided I had to wander
around.
 To feel the coarse cracked walls, old damp
ceiling,
 and the comfort of the old rocking chair lying
on the ground.

 I walked behind you hiding in your shadows.
 Watched slumber unfurl upon you when you lay
asleep.
 I listened to you talk and laugh with your
friends,
 And also heard your thoughts; that in your head;
lay deep.

 At last one evening, when your eyes looked into
mine
 You recognized me; without even saying a word
of surprise
 It was then I understood that humanity was your
façade,
 a pretension because you were another monster
in disguise.

I found solace in your eyes that gleamed of monstrosity.
 I felt warmth linger in the deep gallows of cold heart.
 The emptiness in our eyes sparked a flint in the dark souls.
 Even if the end would be catastrophic, it was a beautiful start.

 You had been where I was, You knew what I was
 You knew I couldn't keep a disguise like you and go around.
 You held my hands and kissed gently on my forehead.
 Your touch could save my world but your kiss burned it to the ground.

 People always said I had no story to tell about myself,
 I had none of my origin and would never have one about my end.
 You saw through my burnt visage and read the story untold
 gave me the freedom so that, beyond worldly boundaries, I could transcend.

The Defeat

Carrying her son around in her arms
 Had always been for her, a source of joy.
 Be it the scorching sun, or the chilly winters
 She never missed a chance to play with her boy.

 She frolicked around the flowery fields with
him,
 played hide & seek amidst the meadows green
and bright.
 And at the end of the day when he got drowsy
and tired,
 carried him on her shoulders and kissed him
goodnight.

 She knit his sweaters early morning before he
woke,
 taught him to read every afternoon, under the
big oak tree.
 Played games with him in the evenings and let
him win,
 so that at night she could watch him sleep,
peaceful and glee.

She brought him up not just like her own son,

but like he were a piece of her own heart.
 Years later her eyes were moist with tears of
joy,
 when he stood before her a man, hale and smart.

 But today, when she has to carry him in her
arms again,
 her heart is filled with agony; eyes red with
tears and pain.
 Her little boy whom she nurtured like a flower
upto this far,
 fell a poor victim to the squalid ravenousness of
War.

 He was the precious jewel she kept close to her
heart,
 never did she let any menacing peril befall him.
 Now she has to fall on to her knees, helpless &
watch the priests,
 lay him in his grave and pray that eternal peace
be upon him.

 At a distance, she could hear sounds of trumpets
& victory processions.
 the people brandishing arms with joy amidst
soup simmering in cauldrons.
 She sat leaning on his gravestone, her gown still
marked with his bloodstains.

Looking at the stars, thinking how much a war could be futile and vain.

The Color Red

He stood still, all by himself in the heavy
downpour.
 The stinging raindrops scalding him like
smouldering coal
 The darkness of the night not able to show a
candle
 To the tenebrosity that resided deep within his
soul

 The sound of his breathing muffled the howling
of the wind.
 The pangs of deprivation in his eyes slowly bid
his sanity adieu.
 Even the Almighty felt a chill slowly run down
his own spine,
 At the sight of the abomination, fate had turned
that man into

 He got down on his knees, one last time to
collect his broken dreams.
 With the rags of his hopes, he wiped off his
tears of colour red,
 All his hatred, all his desperation, he gathered
together in a pile.

And with the untamed fire of his rage, forged a
weapon of desecration,
At the sight of which the heavens bled.

He reached for the stars, armed solely with his
sword of vengeance.
To plunge the blade into the heart of the one
who claimed omnipotence.
Legends say the scorch of the sun melted his
sword, but couldn't scathe his soul.
Unarmed, he stood in front of the Lord, his
malevolent gaze staring a hole.

That day, the God realized that in his world of
black and white,
Existed a deep, dark and vindictive colour of
red.
He need not fear Satan locked away in the
gallows of hell,
But the disillusionment of man when he could
not provide for his family
A cup of milk and a loaf of bread.

Solitude

The rain outside reminds me of something.
Something, I'm hiding deep in my memory.
I cannot remember, I will not remember.
For it will cause me only pain.

Here in my loneliness, I cry, I smile.
Dark is my mind, cold is my heart.
on my wounded knees, I pray,
Pray for nothing.

My god is dead, my hope is broken
but sanity is still mine.
I remember what I used to love
I know what fate took from me.

Time is coming, time is parting
bringing to me what I loved,
& then taking it away with a smile
What lasts is Me, My Solitude & Myself.

A simple laugh for the pain inside,
a gentle smile for all the tears I'm hiding.
for I know pain will slowly swallow me
& tears are as useless as words.

A Lot Remained Unsaid

As my fingers ran through the moist soil,
I felt a familiar fragrance that made me
remember.
That crimson smile and those cheery laughs,
Which warmed up one's heart in the cold of
December.

It was a fragrance that made the roses envy,
It was a fragrance that made the lilies blush.
It was a fragrance that humbled all the essence,
And a fragrance that could make one's heart
rush.

I sat down on the ground, leaning against a tree.
Thinking about the times when these valleys
echoed
With your melodic voice singing songs of joy
In the sun-shone days or the nights that snowed.

I remember standing by the windows for long
Watching you tend the flowers under the sky
deep blue.

Though I started to feel my fondness for you to grow
Silently Fate knew how I close was I to losing you.

The other day you were not to be seen
The grass turned yellow, and the flowers did wither.
Longing for you to breathe life back onto them
All started turning gloomy and grey down hither.

I wandered around hoping to find you again
Shattered and scared for you, I became.
Lost in despair when I fell to my knees,
With a rush of wind your fragrance came.

I knew you were here but not to be seen,
I knew you could see me but didn't want to be found.
I could feel your spirit up in the air
And your grace that still inhabited this forsaken ground.

Those times I stood by the window all day
Watching you through the scope of my gun.
I realized you were that drop of water which could have

Resuscitated this land, arid of humanity and
barren.

I had to kill you, I was meant to kill you
Like the other people of your land, you needed
to die.
I came to this war daily deciding to shoot at
you.
But the more I saw you, the more I loved you,
to bid a goodbye.

And then that day I did lose you.
Lost you somewhere I couldn't find.
That day a lot ended with you for me,
As you were the one thing I had all those days
on my mind.

Today I come back to this place decades later
Then when I first saw you frolicking around the
farms of wheat
The grasses are burnt and the soil's all moist
with red,
But your fragrance still lingers around as I tread
these streets.

They say we won and conquered all lands,
They say it's all over, and we are the mightiest.
I look around and see you aren't with me,

You never could be with me and that pains my
chest.

I will sow those flowers, I will water that grass.
I will plant those trees which birds would nest
with glee.
And while I will sit watching those lambs
stutter around the farms
I will know You will be in the heavens watching
over me.

December Rain!

Waking up from the deep slumber, he had never
felt more tired.
 The darkness around him burned bright in his
eyes,
 While a deafening silence lingered in his house.
 He stood dripping with sweat in the cold night
of December
 Looking at the phone hoping, that to call her, he
would find a reason
 But Only to hear her beautiful voice of treason.

 The movie on tape showed a tiger hunting a
deer and eating its insides.
 He reached his hands to find his heart and found
it hollowed out.
 The wound seemed to be fresh, green and
warm,
 Warmer than her soft hands that had clawed his
heart out.

 He put on his jacket and went walking out in the
streets,
 Where the dark clouds in the skies heavily
rained.

The chilly December rain was warmer than his
cold eyes,
 And neither did the cold winds of the night
cause him any pain.

 He sat on the desolate porch, thoroughly
drenched with rain to his skin,
 When he felt a warm stream trickle down the
back of his neck.
 He turned around to see her dark silhouette
holding a ruddy shining blade,
 "With thy vile blood, I finally avenge my love's
demise", were the last words she spake.

Sometimes

Sometimes I sit by myself all evening
 In the damp corner of the quiet street-side bar.
 An unfinished glass in my hands
 An unfinished tale on my lips
 And burnt pages of my diary, lying by the lit
cigar.

 Sometimes I lock myself out of the world
 Trying to set my inner demons on fire.
 But then I step back, take a look & understand
that
 I would end up burning all my wishes, whims
and desire.

 Sometimes I try to wash my face before I go
out,
 Trying to cleanse it of all the things I have been
blamed.
 But the taint is darker and thicker than blood
 And all that cleansing leaves my hands scarlet
stained.

 I wear white to hide the darkness surrounding
my life,

I fake a laugh and a demeanour to bury the
secret of all my lies.
 But as I walk through the streets deceiving all
those people
 I could sometimes feel a piercing stare,
 Maybe the statues of Gods do have eyes.

 When I cannot bear the damnation any more,
 Sometimes I hide in the darkness of the
moonless night.
 I know the sleepless nights have turned my
instincts frail
 But I have to scourge all hope to put up a fight.

 The fight was against my hopes, my wishes, my
past.
 A fight against the dreams which never became
true.
 When I couldn't take it any more, I ripped out
my insides
 Only to find that my heart still echoed of you!

O Death!

You have a beautiful melody like none other,
 Your charm is beyond any compare.
 You bestow a sense of serenity and repose,
 One would never want to share.

 For once, You confer the solace one's heart
covets.
 Your tranquillity puts all woes at rest.
 The rush of fresh wind gushing along You,
 Fizzles out all fires of agony within one's
breast.

 Your touch can heal the oldest of open wounds,
 Your visage shines too bright for one to stare.
 One falls down to his knees beseeching to
know,
 O Death, why do You take so long to rid one of
his despair!

Reflections

Of all life's gifts, the one that's most profound,
 Is how it shapes and molds us as we grow,
 Reflections in our minds are oft renowned,
 And all that we have seen has helped us know.

 The mirror of experience reflects,
 The highs and lows that we have faced with
grace,
 It shows the paths that we have circumspect,
 And helps us learn from each and every case.

 Through years and decades, we have lived and
learned,
 And all those experiences have shaped our fate,
 Our understanding deepened as we turned,
 And wiser we have grown, more pragmatic and
great.

 In retrospect, we see with clearer sight,
 Reflections of our lives, both dark and bright.